smoothies & juices

for summer

smoothies
& juices
for summer

natural blends to delight and inspire

MARKS &
SPENCER

Marks and Spencer p.l.c.
PO Box 3339
Chester CH99 9QS

shop online
www.marksandspencer.com

Copyright © Exclusive Editions 2006

ISBN: 978-1-84805-519-3

Printed in China

Designed by Talking Design
Photography by Günter Beer
Home Economist Stevan Paul
Additional recipes and text by Linda Doeser

The views expressed in this book are those of the author, but they are general views only and readers are urged to consult a relevant and qualified specialist for individual advice in particular situations. Marks and Spencer p.l.c. and Exclusive Editions Limited hereby exclude all liability to the extent permitted by law for any errors or omissions in this book and for any loss, damage or expense (whether direct or indirect) suffered by a third party relying on any information contained in this book.

NOTES FOR THE READER

This book uses metric and imperial measurements. Follow the same units of measurement throughout; do not mix metric and imperial.

All spoon measurements are level: teaspoons are assumed to be 5 ml, and tablespoons are assumed to be 15 ml.

Unless otherwise stated, milk is assumed to be full fat, eggs and individual vegetables such as potatoes are medium, and pepper is freshly ground black pepper.

Recipes using raw or very lightly cooked eggs should be avoided by infants, the elderly, pregnant women, convalescents and anyone suffering from an illness.

Contents

Introduction

DRINKING FLAVOURED MILK AND FRUIT JUICES IS CERTAINLY NOTHING NEW, BUT TODAY'S GENERATION OF SMOOTHIES AND JUICES REFLECT A LEVEL OF SOPHISTICATION TYPICAL OF THE TWENTY-FIRST CENTURY LIFESTYLE. CONTEMPORARY TASTES TOGETHER WITH A CONCERN FOR HEALTHIER OPTIONS IN THE DIET HAVE RESULTED IN INNOVATIVE COMBINATIONS OF FLAVOURS PLUS THE USE OF FRESH INGREDIENTS.

Smoothies trace their ancestry back to the milkshakes of the last century and they are probably descendants of the eighteenth-century milk punch. To begin with milk was flavoured with a variety of spirits, brandy being particularly popular, then the milkshake – milk whisked with ice cream – was invented. This was further enhanced with the addition of extra flavourings, such as fruit. With the phenomenal development of artificial flavourings and colourings, the milkshake degenerated into a chemical mix that had never been near a strawberry or banana and was often sickly sweet. It finally came of age with the smoothie, usually based on milk or other dairy products and flavoured with fresh fruit or vegetables or a combination of both. Herbs and spices often add extra zing to the mix, appealing to adult palates as well as to children and young people.

Fruit and to a lesser extent vegetable juices have always been valued thirst quenchers. Understandably, easily squeezed fruits, such as oranges, were the most common and, generally, the juice was served on its own. Sometimes, other flavourings were incorporated, perhaps the most familiar being a dash of Worcestershire sauce in tomato juice. Gradually, the ease and convenience of commercially produced juices made fresh juice virtually obsolete in most homes. However, one positive thing that happened at the same time was that in their search for a greater share of the market, manufacturers started to produce mixed juices, such as a combination of tropical fruits. Now, with our desire for more subtle flavours and our nutritional awareness, fresh fruit and vegetable juices, often in the form of exotic 'cocktails', have returned to the domestic kitchen.

Just because we know what is good for us doesn't mean that we always do what is right. For example, we all know that nutritionists recommend five portions of fruit and vegetables a day and most people recognize that it is important to start the day with breakfast. However, life is lived in the fast lane these days and it is difficult to fit in shopping and cooking with the demands of work and family life. Smoothies and juices can make a considerable contribution to resolving this dilemma. They can be made in minutes, so saving precious time in the kitchen. They are full of nutrients and count towards the essential 'five a day'. Many are positive powerhouses and provide a real energy boost first thing in the morning or at any time when you feel that you are running out of steam.

Happily, smoothies and juices are the exception to the popular 'rule' that it won't do you any good if it doesn't taste nasty. On the contrary, the flavours burst deliciously in the mouth, whether sweet or savoury. Teenagers regard them as 'cool', so they are an argument-free, easy alternative to sugar-packed fizzy drinks. Kids – even those who loathe vegetables and have to be cajoled into eating a piece of fruit – love them, especially modern milkshakes, which have been reinvented in the wake of the smoothie. For those who don't want alcoholic drinks, they offer an exciting and adult alternative at social gatherings. They can play a useful role in a calorie-controlled diet and may help anyone trying to give up smoking without gaining weight by substituting a sweet-eating habit.

The recipes in this book include a wide range of both sweet and savoury treats and are divided into five chapters. 'Energy Explosion' is the one to turn to in the morning when you need to kick-start the day or when you're pushed for time and simply can't fit making a snack into your schedule. 'Health Booster' is packed with recipes for maximizing your well-being, offering easy and tasty ways to revitalize your looks and refresh a sluggish system. These smoothies and juices are great for keeping you in tip-top condition and are both tempting and nutritious for anyone recovering from an illness. The astonishing range of thirst-quenching and refreshing juices in 'Juicy Joy' is indeed a colourful and luscious delight that will spoil you for choice. When your energy is flagging and the day begins to drag, turn to 'Perfect Pick-me-ups' for a timely reviver. Finally, 'Super Shakes' is for children of all ages with both family favourites and great new ideas.

Fruit

FRUIT FORMS THE BASIS OF THE MAJORITY OF SMOOTHIES AND JUICES,

ALTHOUGH VEGETABLES ALSO PLAY AN IMPORTANT ROLE.

Apple: a good source of dietary fibre, apples contain some vitamin A and C. Eating apples have a natural sweetness and juiciness, especially Braeburn, Gala, Orleans Reinette, Red Delicious and Worcester Pearmain. Choose apples that smell fragrant and avoid any damaged specimens. Apples combine well with berries, carrots and other orchard fruits.

Banana: packed with energy and extremely nutritious, bananas are a rich source of niacin, riboflavin and potassium and contain vitamins A and C. They combine well with berries, nuts, stone fruits and other tropical fruits. The small Lady Finger or Sugar bananas are especially sweet. Always use ripe bananas for smoothies and shakes.

Blueberry: a rich source of vitamin C and also containing iron, blueberries are sweeter than the native bilberries, but these may be substituted. Choose plump berries with a characteristic bloom. Frozen blueberries can also be used in smoothies.

Grapefruit: one grapefruit will provide more than the adult daily requirement of vitamin C. The juice is particularly refreshing but often quite sour. The variety Sweetie does not require extra sweetening and both pink and ruby grapefruit tend to be sweeter than white ones. Choose firm, ripe fruits as they will be juicy.

Guava: exceptionally high in vitamin C, guavas are also a good source of niacin and potassium. There are several varieties, all with a sweet-sour flavour and aromatic flesh. They combine well with apples and other tropical fruit.

Kiwi fruit: these are very rich in vitamin C and also contain vitamin E. The seeds are edible. Choose plump fruit which will be juicy. The enzymes in kiwi fruit will cause dairy products to curdle. They combine well with berries and other tropical fruit.

Mango: a good source of vitamins A and C, mangoes also contain beta-carotene. There are thousands of varieties – Bombay is particularly juicy. Choose fragrant fruit that yields when gently pressed. Mangoes go well with melon, coconut and other tropical fruits.

Melon: as they have a high water content, melons are great for smoothies and juices. Orange-fleshed varieties contain carotene, an antioxidant that can help protect against some diseases. Most varieties are suitable for making drinks – Cantaloupe and Charentais, both orange-fleshed varieties, are especially fragrant and flavourful. Buy fruit that feels heavy and smells sweet. Melon combines well with berries, pineapple, cucumber, mint, ginger and other varieties of melon.

Orange: all citrus fruits, including tangerines and their hybrids, are very rich in vitamin C. Only sweet oranges are suitable for drinks (bitter varieties are used for marmalade and savoury sauces). An ideal variety is Valencia, which is very juicy and has few pips, and blood oranges provide extra colour. Avoid damaged or shrivelled oranges as they will be dry. Oranges combine well with berries, stone fruits and other citrus fruit.

Passion fruit: a source of vitamins A and C, passion fruit has a sweet-sour flavour. The seeds are edible but the pulp may be sieved. Choose firm, slightly wrinkled fruit that feels heavy and do not store in the refrigerator. Passion fruit combines well with berries and other tropical fruits.

Peach: a source of vitamins A, B and C, peaches have a natural sweetness. They may be white or yellow – choose whichever you prefer. Always buy ripe peaches (they do not ripen after picking) and do not store for more than 2 days. Peel and stone them before use. They combine well with nuts and most other fruit, especially raspberries.

Pear: an orchard fruit containing some riboflavin, potassium and vitamins A and C, pears come in a wide variety of shapes and sizes. Especially juicy varieties include Anjou, Comice, Packham's and Williams Bon Chrétien. Buy ripe fruit but avoid any that is squashy. Pears go well with most other fruit.

Pineapple: rich in vitamin C, pineapples also contain an enzyme that breaks down protein so the juice is an aid to digestion. It is a sweet fruit with a slightly acerbic edge to it. There are many varieties, not usually sold by name. Choose a plump fruit and test for ripeness by gently pulling out one of the bottom leaves. Do not store it in the refrigerator. It combines well with melon, other tropical fruit, coconut and tropical spices, such as ginger and cinnamon.

Raspberry: a good source of vitamin C, niacin, riboflavin and potassium, raspberries have long been credited with healing properties. There are many varieties, all of which are fragrant and juicy. Buy evenly coloured fruit and do not store for longer than 2 days. Raspberries combine particularly well with peaches and also with melon and other berries.

Strawberry: probably the world's most popular soft fruit, strawberries contain iron, potassium and vitamins B and C. There are many different varieties and all are sweet and succulent, especially if locally grown. Choose ripe fruit that has not been squashed. Don't wash strawberries as they will become waterlogged and do not store for more than 24 hours. Strawberries combine well with peaches, bananas, pineapples and other berries.

Watermelon: containing some vitamin B and C, watermelons have a very high water content and a refreshing flavour. Sugar Baby is a particularly sweet variety. Choose firm fruit that does not sound hollow when tapped. Watermelon combines well with lemon, orange, grapefruit and other melons.

Essential Equipment

MOST OF THE EQUIPMENT REQUIRED FOR MAKING SMOOTHIES, JUICES AND SHAKES WILL ALREADY EXIST IN ANY REASONABLY WELL-STOCKED KITCHEN. NO SPECIALIST EXPENSIVE TOOLS ARE REQUIRED, ALTHOUGH YOU MIGHT LIKE TO CHOOSE SOME THAT SPEED THINGS UP OR MAKE LIFE A LITTLE EASIER. REMEMBER THAT YOU WILL NEED TO HAVE ADEQUATE STORAGE SPACE FOR ANY EXTRA EQUIPMENT WHEN IT IS NOT IN USE.

Blender

This is the most expensive piece of equipment you will require for making smoothies, juices and milkshakes and is a worthwhile investment in any kitchen. A detachable goblet fits on to a base that houses the motor. Small blades in the goblet whirl around chopping finely or reducing ingredients to a purée. There is usually a feeder tube or removable cover that allows you to add ingredients, usually a liquid, while the motor is running. Most blenders have at least 2 speeds and all modern domestic models have safety features. Food processors or liquidizers can also be used.

Juicers

Although the recipes featured in this book do not require an electric juicer the investment in one could be very worthwhile. These machines offer you a fast and efficient way to produce good quantities of juice with the minimum of effort. Simply chop the fruit or vegetables into small enough pieces to fit in the juicer, turn it on and watch as the juicer automatically separates the juice from the pulp and skin leaving you with a clean and tasty glass of juice. On some models you don't even have to peel or core the fruit!

Chopping boards

Always keep a separate board for preparing fruit and vegetables and never use it for poultry, meat or fish. Wooden boards look attractive and do the least damage to knife blades. They cannot be sterilized but this is not an important consideration for one kept exclusively for fruit and vegetables. Polyethylene boards, which come in a range of colours, can be sterilized and are dishwasher-proof. They have rough surfaces to prevent both food and board from slipping.

Citrus press

A classic dome-shaped lemon squeezer is easiest to use and inexpensive. A cone-shaped press is very efficient.

Corer

Short and long corers are available. You simply push the circular cutting edge through the centre of the fruit or vegetable and withdraw the core in the cylinder. As fruit and vegetables are usually sliced or chopped for drinks, you can remove the cores of such fruit as apples with a paring knife at the same time.

Grater

A standard box grater is suitable for all kinds of grating and slicing, including grating citrus rind, the most likely use when preparing drinks. A special citrus grater, made from acid-resistant stainless steel, is also available.

Knives

A range of cook's knives is essential for any type of food preparation including making drinks. It is better to buy them separately than as a set, testing the balance of each by holding it in your hand. Heavy, but well-balanced knives are more efficient and easier to use than light ones. A cook's knife, with a wide, curved blade 20–25 cm/8–10 inches long, is an all-purpose tool and can be used for hefty tasks, such as slicing fruit and vegetables as well as light ones, such as chopping herbs. A utility knife is a slightly smaller version with a 13–18-cm/5–7-inch-long blade and is useful for light slicing and chopping. A paring knife, with a similar shaped blade 8–10 cm/3^{1}/$_{4}$-4 inches long, is ideal for peeling and scraping fruit and vegetables and for slicing and chopping small items. It is very useful for preparing ingredients, such as oranges, peaches and root ginger, for smoothies.

Store knives in a knife block rather than a drawer where they will be a danger to fingers and liable to damage. A steel or knife sharpener helps keep them in good condition.

Sieves and strainers

A range of different sizes is useful in any kitchen. Use a nylon sieve for acidic fruits as metal may taint the flavour.

Vegetable peelers

There are three basic types – swivel, V-shaped and Y-shaped – all of which make it easier than using a knife to peel fruit and vegetables thinly. Which type you choose is a matter of taste but left-handed people should check that the sharp edge works for them or buy a special left-handed version.

Top 10 Tips for Smoothie Success

1 Use the freshest possible, ripe ingredients. Over-ripe or damaged fruit will not improve by being made into a smoothie.

2 Use fruit and vegetables that are in season and, preferably, locally grown for the best flavour and greatest natural sweetness.

3 Don't prepare fruit and vegetables in advance, as they will start to dry out and lose their juiciness. Some vitamins are quickly destroyed on exposure to air so this would also reduce the nutritional value – one of the great benefits of smoothies.

4 Smoothies are best served chilled, but adding ice will dilute them. Keep milk and other dairy products in the refrigerator until required. Chill the glasses before you make the smoothie. If you want to add ice to the blender, crack it first to avoid damaging the blades. Put ice cubes in a plastic bag, wrap it in a clean tea towel and hit with a hard object or swing against a hard wall that won't be damaged.

5 When adding strongly flavoured spices, such as ground ginger or chillies, err on the side of caution. Add half the suggested quantity, taste and add more if you like.

6 Never overfill the blender goblet; check the manufacturer's instructions for the maximum capacity for your particular model. Overfilling may result in liquid spilling out of the top and/or the ingredients being inadequately combined. About half full is best for smoothies, so if necessary, make them in batches.

7 To save time and for even mixing, chop ingredients into pieces about the same size. They don't have to be finely diced but should be fairly small.

8 When measuring spoonfuls of honey, the most popular sweetener for smoothies, dip the spoon in hot water first. This makes it easier to get all the honey into the mixture rather than leaving half of it behind. This is also a good idea with ice cream scoops if you are using ice cream straight from the freezer for shakes.

9 Use fresh herbs whenever possible, but if the one you require is not available, substitute a similar one or use frozen herbs. Dried herbs do not work in smoothies.

10 Don't be afraid to experiment. Try substituting different berries, a flavoured yogurt for natural or, if you are cutting down on your intake of fat, skimmed milk for full-fat.

Top 10 Benefits of Smoothies & Juices

1 Using fresh fruit and vegetables in prime condition ensures optimum nutritional value.

2 Smoothies are an easy and delicious way to increase your intake of fruit and vegetables – a direct way towards a healthier diet for all the family.

3 There are no artificial flavours, colours or preservatives, some of which are known to have adverse effects on people with allergies and on children.

4 Fruit and some vegetables, particularly carrots and beetroot, are naturally sweet so smoothies and juices are an easy way to reduce sugar intake without compromising taste.

5 They take hardly any time to make, yet provide an instant energy boost and quench your thirst.

6 They offer a tasty and interesting alternative to commercial products, cost less, are usually healthier and can be adapted to your personal taste.

7 You can drink them any time of day from breakfast to bedtime and they provide a far better, longer-lasting and healthier snack when your energy is flagging than crisps, chocolate or biscuits.

8 They're a great way of using up odd pieces of fruit – the last banana in the bowl or a few grapes left on the stem – providing they are still in good condition.

9 You know exactly what ingredients have been used, so there are no unpleasant surprises or hidden quantities of saturated fats or sugar.

10 They taste fabulous!

Energy Explosion

Banana Breakfast Shake

GET YOUR DAY OFF TO A HEALTHY START WITH THIS QUICK BUT NUTRITIOUS BANANA SHAKE. BANANAS ARE A GREAT SOURCE OF POTASSIUM WHICH IS SAID TO PLAY A ROLE IN CONTROLLING HIGH BLOOD PRESSURE.

SERVES 2

2 RIPE BANANAS
200 ML/7 FL OZ LOW-FAT
  NATURAL YOGURT
125 ML/4 FL OZ SKIMMED MILK
1/2 TSP VANILLA ESSENCE

Put the bananas, yogurt, milk and vanilla essence into a food processor and process until smooth.

Serve at once.

Breakfast Bar

THIS FRUITY DRINK PROVIDES A GREAT 'PICK-ME-UP' AT ANY TIME OF THE DAY
AND IS PERFECT FOR GIVING AN ENERGY BOOST FIRST THING IN THE MORNING.

 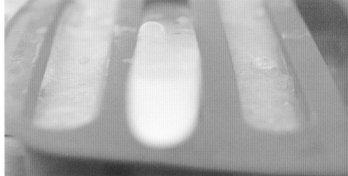

SERVES 4

400 G/14 OZ CANNED GRAPEFRUIT
   AND ORANGE SEGMENTS
4 TBSP LEMON JUICE
3 TBSP LIME JUICE
425 ML/15 FL OZ ORANGE
   JUICE, CHILLED

Tip the canned fruit and the can juices into the blender. Add the lemon,
lime and orange juice and process until smooth.

Pour into chilled glasses and serve.

Rise & Shine Juice

Vegetables may not be the first thing you think of for a breakfast drink, but this juice is packed with nutrients and is a great way to start your 'five-a-day'.

SERVES **1**

4 TOMATOES, QUARTERED
85 G/3 OZ GRATED CARROT
1 TBSP LIME JUICE

Put the tomatoes, carrot and lime juice into a blender and process for a few seconds until smooth.

Place a nylon sieve over a bowl and pour in the tomato mixture. Using a spoon, gently push as much of the liquid through the sieve as possible. Discard any pips and pulp remaining in the sieve.

Pour the juice into a glass and serve immediately.

Breakfast Smoothie

KICK-START YOUR DAY WITH THIS RICH VITAMIN-AND MINERAL-PACKED ENERGIZER.

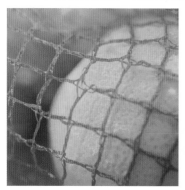

SERVES 2

250 ML/9 FL OZ ORANGE JUICE
125 ML/4 FL OZ NATURAL YOGURT
2 EGGS
2 BANANAS, SLICED AND FROZEN

DECORATION
SLICE OF FRESH BANANA OR
1 SMALL BANANA

Pour the orange juice and yogurt into a food processor and process gently until combined.

Add the eggs and frozen bananas and process until smooth.

Pour the mixture into glasses and decorate with the banana.

Wake Up Sweetie

SWEETIE GRAPEFRUIT AND UGLI FRUIT ARE VERY SIMILAR — A HYBRID OF GRAPEFRUIT, THEY ARE SWEETER AND JUICIER, PERFECT TO WAKE YOU UP IN THE MORNING.

SERVES 2

3 LARGE RIPE SWEETIE GRAPEFRUIT
  OR UGLI FRUIT
150 ML/5 FL OZ SPARKLING WATER
1 TBSP FLOWERY RUNNY HONEY
  (OPTIONAL)

DECORATION
SOME SLICES OF LIME OR
  PEELED KIWI FRUIT
2 TBSP LOW FAT YOGURT

Halve and squeeze the fruit into two glasses.

Add water and honey if liked.

Serve with a slice or two of lime or kiwi, floated on the surface and topped with a tablespoon of yogurt.

American Berry Smoothie

THIS ENERGIZING SMOOTHIE IS A GREAT WAY TO KICK-START THE DAY. ADD 1–2 TSP OF CLEAR HONEY IF YOU PREFER YOUR SMOOTHIES A LITTLE SWEETER.

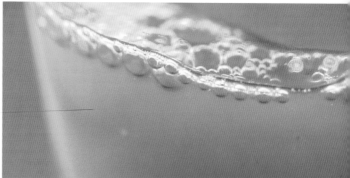

SERVES 2

175 G/6 OZ BLUEBERRIES
150 ML/5 FL OZ CRANBERRY JUICE
150 ML/5 FL OZ NATURAL YOGURT
HONEY, TO TASTE (OPTIONAL)

Put the blueberries and cranberry juice into a blender and process for 1–2 minute until smooth.

Add the natural yogurt and process briefly to combine. Taste and add honey if you like. Process briefly again until thoroughly blended.

Pour into chilled glasses with straws and serve.

Tropical Watermelon Smoothie

THE PERFECT CHOICE FOR A SUMMERY DAY – IT WILL BOOST YOUR VITALITY AND
QUENCH YOUR THIRST FROM SUNRISE TO SUNSET.

SERVES 2

1 WATERMELON WEDGE,
  ABOUT 600 G/1 LB 5 OZ
2 SMALL BANANAS, PREFERABLY
  LADY FINGER
225 ML/8 FL OZ COCONUT CREAM

Remove and discard the seeds from the watermelon, then cut the flesh off t
rind and chop coarsely. Peel and slice the bananas.

Put the watermelon, bananas and coconut cream in a blender and process
until combined.

Pour into chilled glasses and serve.

Raspberry & Strawberry Smoothie

POSSIBLY TWO OF THE MOST POPULAR FRUITS COME TOGETHER IN THIS DELICIOUS MIX — A TASTE SENSATION.

SERVES **2–4**

55 G/2 OZ RASPBERRIES
55 G/2 OZ STRAWBERRIES, HALVED
225 ML/8 FL OZ CRÈME FRAÎCHE
225 ML/8 FL OZ MILK
1 TSP ALMOND ESSENCE (OPTIONAL)
2–3 TBSP CLEAR HONEY, TO TASTE

Press the raspberries through a nylon sieve into a bowl using the back of a spoon. Discard the seeds in the sieve.

Put the raspberry purée, strawberries, crème fraîche, milk and almond essence (if using) into a blender and process until smooth and combined.

Pour the smoothie into chilled glasses, stir in honey to taste and serve.

Ruby Anyday

TOO GOOD JUST FOR TUESDAYS, THIS IS RUBY ANYDAY.

SERVES 2

1 LARGE RIPE PINK OR RUBY GRAPEFRUIT
100 ML/3¹/2 FL OZ ICE-COLD WATER
100 G/3¹/2 OZ GREEK YOGURT
1 TBSP FLOWERY CLEAR HONEY,
   SUCH AS ACACIA

DECORATION
SLICES OF PINK OR RUBY GRAPEFRUIT

Quarter the grapefruit, then pull off the peel and as much pith as possible. Discard any seeds.

Put the grapefruit and water into a food processor and process until smooth. Add the yogurt and honey and process again until combined.

Pour into glasses, decorate with slices of grapefruit and serve.

Blueberry Thrill

BLUEBERRIES ARE STILL A MUCH UNDERRATED PLEASURE. IN THIS SMOOTHIE THEIR RAW, TART SWEETNESS IS ENHANCED BY THE YOGURT.

SERVES 2

100 ML/3¹/₂ FL OZ GREEK YOGURT
100 ML/3¹/₂ FL OZ WATER
125 G/4¹/₂ OZ FROZEN BLUEBERRIES

DECORATION
WHOLE FROZEN BLUEBERRIES

Put the yogurt, water and blueberries into a food processor and process until smooth.

Pour into glasses and top with whole frozen blueberries.

Orange & Strawberry Cream

THE IMPECCABLE COMBINATION OF FRESH FLAVOURS MAKES THIS ONE OF THE
MOST POPULAR SMOOTHIES.

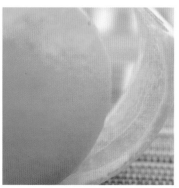

SERVES 2

125 ML/4 FL OZ NATURAL YOGURT

175 ML/6 FL OZ STRAWBERRY YOGURT

175 ML/6 FL OZ ORANGE JUICE

175 G/6 OZ FROZEN STRAWBERRIES

1 BANANA, SLICED AND FROZEN

DECORATION

SLICES OF ORANGE AND WHOLE FRESH
  STRAWBERRIES ON COCKTAIL STICKS

Pour the natural and strawberry yogurts into a food processor and process gently. Add the orange juice and process until combined.

Add the strawberries and banana and process until smooth.

Pour the mixture into tall glasses and decorate with slices of orange and whole strawberries on a cocktail stick.

Fruit Kefir

SUBSTITUTE THE PEACH YOGURT FOR A FLAVOUR OF YOUR CHOICE TO TRY A DIFFERENT OPTION OF THIS DELICIOUS BLEND.

SERVES 4

1 BANANA

115 G/4 OZ STRAWBERRIES, HALVED

225 ML/8 FL OZ PEACH YOGURT

2 TBSP CLEAR HONEY

225 ML/8 FL OZ APPLE JUICE, CHILLED

Peel the banana and slice it directly into the blender.

Add the strawberries, yogurt and honey and process until smooth. With th motor running, pour in the apple juice through the hole in the lid.

Pour into chilled glasses and serve.

Berry Smoothie

THE BERRIES GIVE THIS SMOOTHIE A RICH SHADE OF PINK, MAKING IT A GREAT TREAT TO SERVE AT KIDS' PARTIES.

SERVES 2

300 ML/10 FL OZ FULL-FAT MILK
  OR SOYA MILK
2 TBSP NATURAL YOGURT
1 TBSP MAPLE SYRUP
3 BLACKBERRIES
50 G/1³/4 OZ BLUEBERRIES
25 G/1 OZ BLACKCURRANTS

DECORATION
ROASTED SESAME SEEDS

Place all the ingredients in a blender or food processor and process until combined and frothy.

Pour into tall glasses, sprinkle the roasted sesame seeds over the top and serve immediately.

Almond & Banana Smoothie

THIS IS A GREAT SMOOTHIE FOR THOSE FOLLOWING A DAIRY-FREE DIET, BUT THERE IS CERTAINLY NO COMPROMISE ON TASTE.

SERVES 3–4

125 G/4^{1}/$_{2}$ OZ WHOLE BLANCHED
  ALMONDS
600 ML/1 PINT DAIRY-FREE MILK
2 RIPE BANANAS, HALVED
1 TSP NATURAL VANILLA EXTRACT
GROUND CINNAMON, FOR SPRINKLING

Put the almonds into a food processor and process until very finely chopped. Add the milk, bananas and vanilla extract and blend until smooth and creamy.

Pour into glasses and sprinkle with cinnamon.

Banana, Peach & Strawberry Smoothie

THIS SMOOTHIE REQUIRES A LITTLE PREPARATION AS YOU WILL NEED TO PEEL THE PEACH, BUT THE RESULT IS WELL WORTH IT.

 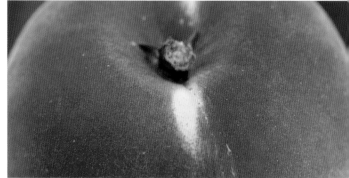

SERVES 2

300 ML/10 FL OZ FULL-FAT MILK
   OR SOYA MILK
2 TBSP NATURAL YOGURT
1 TBSP MAPLE SYRUP
1/2 PEELED AND SLICED BANANA
1/2 STONED, PEELED AND
   CHOPPED PEACH
3 HULLED STRAWBERRIES

Place all the ingredients in a blender or food processor and process until combined and frothy.

Pour into glasses and serve immediately.

Orchard Fruit Smoothie

THE VERY BRIEF COOKING OF THE FRUIT JUST MELLOWS THE FLAVOURS AND ALLOWS THE COLOURS FROM THE DAMSONS AND PLUMS TO SEEP INTO THE APPLES AND PEARS.

SERVES 2

1 RIPE PEAR, PEELED AND
  QUARTERED
1 APPLE, PEELED AND QUARTERED
2 LARGE RED OR DARK PLUMS,
  HALVED AND STONED
4 RIPE DAMSONS, HALVED AND
  STONED
200 ML/7 FL OZ WATER

DECORATION
SLICES OF APPLE OR PEAR

Put the pear, apple, plums, damsons and water into a small saucepan. Cove
tightly, set over a medium heat and bring slowly to the boil. Take off the h
and allow to cool. Chill.

Put the fruit and water into a food processor and process until smooth.

Pour into glasses, decorate with slices of apple or pear and serve.

Melon & Pineapple Crush

When you are feeling jaded, this glorious pairing of sweet and tart flavours will perk you up and give you a boost.

SERVES 2

100 ML/3¹/₂ FL OZ PINEAPPLE JUICE
4 TBSP ORANGE JUICE
125 G/4¹/₂ OZ GALIA MELON,
    CUT INTO CHUNKS
140 G/5 OZ FROZEN PINEAPPLE
    CHUNKS
4 ICE CUBES

DECORATION
SLICES OF GALIA MELON

Pour the pineapple juice and orange juice into a food processor and process gently until combined.

Add the melon, pineapple chunks and ice cubes and process until a slushy consistency has been reached.

Pour the mixture into glasses and decorate with slices of melon.

Serve at once.

Carrot & Red Pepper Booster

THIS DYNAMIC COMBINATION OF FLAVOURS WILL FIRE UP YOUR SYSTEM AND BOOST YOUR ENERGY LEVELS.

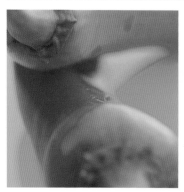 

SERVES 2

250 ML/9 FL OZ CARROT JUICE
250 ML/9 FL OZ TOMATO JUICE
2 LARGE RED PEPPERS, DESEEDED
  AND ROUGHLY CHOPPED
1 TBSP LEMON JUICE
FRESHLY GROUND BLACK PEPPER

Pour the carrot juice and tomato juice into a food processor and process gently until combined.

Add the red peppers and lemon juice. Season with plenty of freshly ground black pepper and process until smooth.

Pour the mixture into glasses, add straws and serve.

Tomato Blazer

TANGY AND A LITTLE BIT HOT, THIS IS A JUICE WITH A BIT OF GET-UP-AND-GO!

SERVES 2

500 ML/18 FL OZ TOMATO JUICE
DASH OF WORCESTERSHIRE SAUCE
1 SMALL RED CHILLI, DESEEDED
AND CHOPPED
1 SPRING ONION, TRIMMED AND
CHOPPED
6 ICE CUBES

DECORATION
2 LONG, THIN RED CHILLIES,
CUT INTO FLOWERS

To make the chilli flowers, use a sharp knife to make six cuts along each chilli. Place the point of the knife about 1 cm/¹/₂ inch from the stalk end and cut towards the tip. Put the chillies in a bowl of iced water and leave them for 25–30 minutes, or until they have spread out into flower shapes.

Put the tomato juice and Worcestershire sauce into a food processor and process gently until combined. Add the chopped chilli, spring onion and ice cubes and process until smooth.

Pour the mixture into glasses and garnish with the chilli flowers.

Vegetable Cocktail

THIS SAVOURY COCKTAIL COMBINES ALL THE GOODNESS OF FRESH VEGETABLES IN ONE GLASS.

SERVES 2

125 ML/4 FL OZ CARROT JUICE

500 G/1 LB 2 OZ TOMATOES, SKINNED, DESEEDED AND ROUGHLY CHOPPED

1 TBSP LEMON JUICE

4 CELERY STICKS, TRIMMED AND SLICED

4 SPRING ONIONS, TRIMMED AND ROUGHLY CHOPPED

25 G/1 OZ FRESH PARSLEY

25 G/1 OZ FRESH MINT

DECORATION

2 LEAFY CELERY STICKS

Put the carrot juice, tomatoes and lemon juice into a food processor and process gently until combined.

Add the sliced celery along with the spring onions, parsley and mint and process until smooth.

Pour the mixture into glasses and garnish with leafy celery sticks.

Serve at once.

Health Booster

Sweet & Sour Smoothie

Boost your immune system and help counteract the effects of the passing years with this delicious and colourful smoothie.

SERVES 2

225 ML/8 FL OZ FRESHLY SQUEEZED
  ORANGE JUICE
175 G/6 OZ COOKED BEETROOT,
  CHOPPED
5 TBSP NATURAL YOGURT
SALT (OPTIONAL)

DECORATION
CHOPPED BEETROOT

Put the orange juice, beetroot and natural yogurt into a blender and add 150 m 5 fl oz of water. Process until smooth and thoroughly combined.

Pour the smoothie into a chilled jug and stir in salt to taste (if using).

Decorate with chopped beetroot and serve.

Papaya & Banana Smoothie

THIS PACKS A REAL NUTRITIONAL PUNCH, YET IS ESPECIALLY EASY TO DIGEST,

SO IT'S THE PERFECT DRINK FOR ANYONE RECOVERING FROM ILLNESS OR FATIGUE.

SERVES 2

1 PAPAYA

JUICE OF 1 LIME

1 LARGE BANANA

350 ML/12 FL OZ FRESHLY

  SQUEEZED ORANGE JUICE

1/4 TSP GROUND GINGER

Halve the papaya and scoop out and discard the grey-black seeds. Scoop out the flesh and chop coarsely, then toss with the lime juice. Peel and slice the banana.

Put the papaya, banana, orange juice and ginger in a blender and process until thoroughly combined.

Pour into chilled glasses and serve.

Detox Special

WHEN YOUR HAIR IS LANK, YOUR SKIN LOOKS DULL AND YOU JUST DON'T FEEL YOURSELF, A RESTORATIVE — AND DELICIOUS — INTAKE OF VITAMINS A AND C IS JUST WHAT THE DOCTOR ORDERED.

SERVES 2

1 MANGO
4 KIWI FRUIT
350 ML/12 FL OZ PINEAPPLE JUICE
4 FRESH MINT LEAVES

Cut the mango into 2 thick slices as close to the stone as possible. Scoop o the flesh and chop coarsely. Cut off any flesh adhering to the stone. Peel th kiwi fruit with a sharp knife and chop the flesh.

Put the mango, kiwi fruit, pineapple juice and mint leaves in a blender and process until thoroughly combined.

Pour into chilled glasses and serve.

Apple & Celery Revitalizer

GIVE YOUR SPIRITS A LIFT AND YOUR HEART A BOOST WITH THIS TASTY VITALITY DRINK. IT IS ALSO REPUTED TO BE SOMETHING OF A HANGOVER CURE.

SERVES 2

1 EATING APPLE, PEELED, CORED
  AND DICED

115 G/4 OZ CELERY, CHOPPED

600 ML/1 PINT MILK

PINCH OF SUGAR (OPTIONAL)

SALT (OPTIONAL)

DECORATION

STRIPS OF CELERY

Put the apple, celery and milk in a blender and process until thoroughly combin

Stir in a pinch of sugar and some salt if you like.

Pour into chilled glasses, decorate with strips of celery and serve.

Banana & Strawberry Smoothie

SIMPLE BUT DELICIOUS, THE STRAWBERRY MAKES YET ANOTHER APPEARANCE IN THIS

CLASSIC COMBINATION.

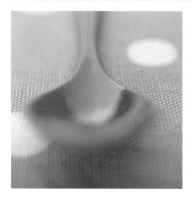 

SERVES 2

1 BANANA, SLICED

85 G/3 OZ FRESH STRAWBERRIES,
  HULLED

150 G/5 1/2 OZ LOW-FAT
  NATURAL YOGURT

Put the banana, strawberries and yogurt into a blender and process for a fe
seconds until smooth.

Pour into glasses and serve immediately.

Tropical Smoothie

PINEAPPLE AND PAPAYA ARE RICH IN ANTIOXIDANTS AND CONTAIN

DIGESTIVE-SYSTEM STIMULATING ENZYMES.

SERVES 2

1 RIPE PAPAYA, PEELED, STONED AND
CHOPPED

1/2 FRESH PINEAPPLE, PEELED
AND CHOPPED

150 ML/5 FL OZ SOYA MILK

300 ML/10 FL OZ SOYA YOGURT

DECORATION
CHOPPED PINEAPPLE

Place all the ingredients in a juicer or blender and process until smooth.

Pour into glasses, decorate with chopped pineapple and serve.

Apple, Carrot & Cucumber Juice

THIS DRINK IS PACKED WITH ANTIOXIDANTS AND SOLUBLE FIBRE, AND THE

DIURETIC PROPERTIES OF CUCUMBER AND CARROT HELP RELIEVE FLUID RETENTION.

 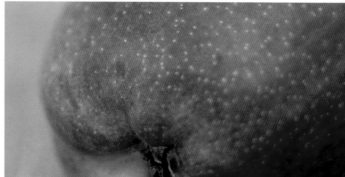

SERVES **1**

1 APPLE, UNPEELED, CORED
  AND CHOPPED
1 CARROT, PEELED AND CHOPPED
1/2 CUCUMBER, CHOPPED

DECORATION
PIECES OF CARROT, CUCUMBER
  AND APPLE ON A COCKTAIL STICK

Place the ingredients in a juicer or blender and process.

Pour into a glass. Put the pieces of carrot, cucumber and apple on to a cocktail stick and set on top of the glass. Serve.

Blueberry Dazzler

SWEET, SHARP, FRAGRANT, RICH AND CREAMY – THIS IS PURE MAGIC IN A GLASS.

SERVES 2

175 ML/6 FL OZ APPLE JUICE

125 ML/4 FL OZ NATURAL YOGURT

1 BANANA, SLICED AND FROZEN

175 G/6 OZ FROZEN BLUEBERRIES

DECORATION

WHOLE FRESH BLUEBERRIES ON
  COCKTAIL STICKS

Pour the apple juice into a food processor. Add the yogurt and process until smoot

Add the banana and half of the blueberries and process well, then add the
remaining blueberries and process until smooth.

Pour the mixture into tall glasses.

Decorate with whole fresh blueberries on a cocktail stick and serve.

Apricot & Orange Smoothie

THIS SMOOTHIE MAKES A GREAT VITAMIN AND MINERAL-PACKED BREAKFAST IN A GLASS.

SERVES 2

250 ML/9 FL OZ BOILING WATER
125 G/4½ OZ DRIED APRICOTS
JUICE OF 4 MEDIUM ORANGES
2 TBSP NATURAL YOGURT
1 TSP SOFT DARK BROWN SUGAR

Put the apricots in a bowl and pour the boiling water over them. Leave to soak overnight.

In the morning, put the apricots and their soaking water into a food process and process until puréed. Add the orange juice to the apricots in the food processor, and process until combined.

Pour into glasses and top with 1 tablespoon of yogurt and a sprinkling of brown sugar.

Berry Booster

SESAME SEEDS ARE AN UNUSUAL ADDITION BUT THEY GIVE THIS SMOOTHIE A LITTLE
SOMETHING EXTRA. SPRINKLE SOME OVER THE TOP TO DECORATE IF DESIRED.

SERVES 1

25 G/1 OZ BLUEBERRIES
85 G/3 OZ RASPBERRIES, THAWED
  IF FROZEN
1 TSP CLEAR HONEY
200 ML/7 FL OZ LIVE OR BIO
  YOGURT
ABOUT 1 HEAPED TBSP CRUSHED ICE
1 TBSP SESAME SEEDS

Put the blueberries into a food processor or blender and process for 1 minu

Add the raspberries, honey and yogurt and process for a further minute.
Add the ice and sesame seeds and process again for a further minute.

Pour into a tall glass and serve immediately.

Guava Goodness

GUAVAS ARE REMARKABLY HIGH IN VITAMIN C AND WHEN BLENDED WITH MILK
PROVIDE A VERY NUTRITIOUS START TO ANY DAY.

SERVES 2

400 G/14 OZ CANNED GUAVAS, DRAINED
250 ML/9 FL OZ ICE-COLD MILK

Place the guavas into a food processor and pour in the milk. Process until well blended.

Strain into glasses to remove the hard seeds. Serve.

Black & Blue

CULTIVATED BLACKBERRIES ARE CONSISTENTLY PLUMP AND JUICY, UNLIKE THEIR
HEDGEROW COUSINS, WHICH CAN BE SUBSTITUTED IF YOU HAVE A GOOD SUPPLY.

SERVES 2

125 G/4^1/$_2$ OZ CULTIVATED
  BLACKBERRIES
125 G/4^1/$_2$ OZ BLUEBERRIES
100 ML/3^1/$_2$ FL OZ ICE-COLD WATER
150 ML/5 FL OZ NATURAL YOGURT

Put the blackberries, blueberries, water and yogurt into a food processor and process until smooth.

Pour into glasses and serve.

Pear & Raspberry Delight

PINK, LIGHT AND FRUITY, THIS REFRESHING SMOOTHIE IS SIMPLY DELICIOUS. IF

YOU DON'T LIKE THE PIPS, YOU CAN USE A SIEVE TO MAKE IT SILKEN SMOOTH.

SERVES 2

2 LARGE RIPE CONFERENCE PEARS
125 G/4¹/₂ OZ FROZEN RASPBERRIES
200 ML/7 FL OZ ICE-COLD WATER
HONEY, TO TASTE

DECORATION
RASPBERRIES ON COCKTAIL STICKS

Peel and quarter the pears, removing the cores. Put into a food processor w
the raspberries and water and process until smooth.

Taste and sweeten with honey if the raspberries are a little sharp.

Pour into glasses and decorate with whole raspberries on a cocktail stick and ser

Mint & Cucumber Refresher

THIS IS GREAT TO SERVE AT A SUMMER PARTY – THE CUCUMBER INSIDE THE GLASS WILL
BE A REAL TALKING POINT!

SERVES 1

FEW SPRIGS MINT

1 TSP CASTER SUGAR

JUICE 1 LIME

2 CM/1 IN PIECE CUCUMBER,
  THINLY SLICED

YOUR FAVOURITE SPARKLING
  WATER, CHILLED

ICE CUBES

Chop a few mint leaves and mix with sugar.

Rub a little lime juice round the rim of a pretty glass and dip in the minted
sugar. Leave to dry.

Mix the rest of the lime juice, cucumber and mint – some chopped and some
whole – in a jug and chill.

To serve, pour the lime and cucumber into the prepared glass and top up with
chilled sparkling water and ice cubes to taste.

Carrot Cocktail

PINEAPPLE AND CARROT ARE A DELICIOUS COMBINATION, PRODUCING A THICK AND REFRESHING DRINK PACKED WITH VITAMINS.

 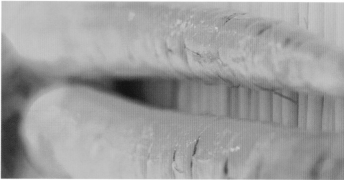

SERVES **1**

85 G/3 OZ RAW CARROTS, PEELED
AND ROUGHLY CHOPPED

1 SLICE PINEAPPLE, ROUGHLY
CHOPPED

1 TSP LEMON JUICE

1 TBSP CLEAR HONEY

ICE

DECORATION

SPRIG OF PARSLEY OR MINT

Place the carrots, pineapple, lemon juice and honey in a blender and whizz for 1–2 minutes until smooth.

Serve over ice with a sprig of parsley or mint.

24 Carrot

PINEAPPLE CONTAINS ENZYMES THAT NOT ONLY AID DIGESTION, BUT CAN
EFFECTIVELY REDUCE INFLAMMATION AND SWELLING.

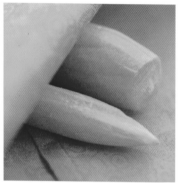 

SERVES 2

HANDFUL OF CRACKED ICE

2 CARROTS, COARSELY CHOPPED

115 G/4 OZ CANNED PINEAPPLE
   PIECES IN JUICE, DRAINED

175 ML/6 FL OZ PINEAPPLE
   JUICE, CHILLED

DECORATION
STRIPS OF CUCUMBER

Put the ice into the blender, add the carrots, pineapple pieces and pineappl
juice and process until slushy.

Pour into chilled glasses and decorate with strips of cucumber.

On The Beat

Beetroot contains no fat, very few calories and is a great source of fibre. Omit the salt if you are being extra healthy.

SERVES 2

175 G/6 OZ COOKED BEETROOT,
  CHOPPED
125 ML/4 FL OZ ORANGE JUICE, CHILLED
5 TBSP NATURAL YOGURT, CHILLED
150 ML/5 FL OZ STILL MINERAL
  WATER, CHILLED
SALT

DECORATION
SLICES OF ORANGE

Put the beetroot, orange juice, yogurt and water into the blender and season to taste with salt.

Process until smooth, then pour into chilled glasses and serve, decorated with slices of orange.

Beetroot, Pear & Spinach Juice

Beetroot stimulates the liver and helps to cleanse the digestive system. The pear adds sweetness and fibre. Spinach contains antioxidants that help to eliminate free radicals.

 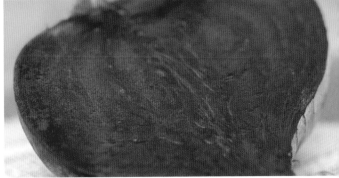

SERVES 1

1 BEETROOT, TRIMMED, PEELED
AND CHOPPED
1 PEAR, CORED AND CHOPPED
25 G/1 OZ FRESH SPINACH LEAVES
FILTERED WATER, TO TASTE

DECORATION
SPINACH LEAF

Place the ingredients in a juicer or blender and process. Dilute with filtered water to taste.

Pour into a glass and decorate with the spinach leaf. Serve.

Carrot & Ginger Energizer

THIS STIMULATING BLEND OF FLAVOURS IS GUARANTEED TO GIVE YOU A BOOST WHEN YOU NEED IT.

SERVES 2

250 ML/9 FL OZ CARROT JUICE

4 TOMATOES, SKINNED, DESEEDED
  AND ROUGHLY CHOPPED

1 TBSP LEMON JUICE

25 G/1 OZ FRESH PARSLEY

1 TBSP GRATED FRESH ROOT GINGER

6 ICE CUBES

125 ML/4 FL OZ WATER

DECORATION

CHOPPED FRESH FLAT-LEAF PARSLEY

Put the carrot juice, tomatoes and lemon juice into a food processor and process gently until combined.

Add the parsley to the food processor along with the ginger and ice cubes. Process until well combined, then pour in the water and process until smoo

Pour the mixture into tall glasses and garnish with chopped fresh parsley.

Serve at once.

Red Pepper Reactor

NOT FOR THE FAINT-HEARTED, THIS FIERY MIX WILL CERTAINLY WAKE YOU UP IF YOU'RE HAVING A MID-MORNING DOZE.

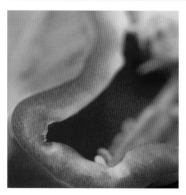

SERVES 2

250 ML/9 FL OZ CARROT JUICE
250 ML/9 FL OZ TOMATO JUICE
2 LARGE RED PEPPERS, DESEEDED
  AND ROUGHLY CHOPPED
1 TBSP LEMON JUICE
FRESHLY GROUND BLACK PEPPER

DECORATION
STRIPS OF SHREDDED CARROT

Pour the carrot juice and tomato juice into a food processor and process gently until combined.

Add the red peppers and lemon juice. Season with plenty of freshly ground black pepper and process until smooth.

Pour the mixture into glasses, decorate with the strips of shredded carrot and serve.

Juicy Joy

Watermelon Whizz

A GREAT FAVOURITE IN GREECE, WHERE ROADSIDE STALLS SELL ENORMOUS
WATERMELONS, THIS SMOOTHIE MAKES THE MOST OF THIS GIGANTIC FRUIT'S JUICINESS.

SERVES 2

1 WEDGE OF WATERMELON,
   WEIGHING ABOUT 350 G/12 OZ
ICE CUBES

DECORATION
SLICES OF WATERMELON

Cut the rind off the watermelon. Chop the watermelon into chunks, discarding any seeds.

Put the watermelon chunks into a food processor and process until smooth

Place the ice cubes in the glasses. Pour the watermelon mixture over the ice and serve decorated with the slices of melon.

Melon & Mango Tango

BOTH WATERMELONS AND CANTALOUPES ARE AMONG THE MOST THIRST-QUENCHING

FRUITS IN THE WORLD AND ARE PERFECT FOR SUMMER DRINKS.

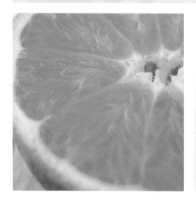 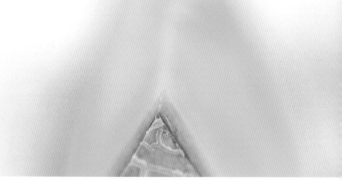

SERVES 2

1 CANTALOUPE MELON, HALVED AND
  DESEEDED
600 ML/1 PINT MANGO JUICE
2 TBSP FRESH ORANGE JUICE

DECORATION
SLICES OF ORANGE

Scoop out the melon flesh with a spoon straight into the blender. Add the mango and orange juices and process until smooth.

Pour into chilled glasses, decorate with slices of orange and serve.

Perky Pineapple

THIS IS A GREAT ENERGY BOOSTER AND IS PACKED FULL OF NUTRIENTS. THE TANGY

TASTE IS EXTREMELY REFRESHING AS WELL.

SERVES 4

HANDFUL OF CRACKED ICE

2 BANANAS

225 ML/8 FL OZ PINEAPPLE JUICE,

   CHILLED

125 ML/4 FL OZ LIME JUICE

DECORATION

SLICES OF PINEAPPLE

Put the cracked ice into the blender. Peel the bananas and slice directly into the blender. Add the pineapple and lime juice and process until smooth.

Pour into chilled glasses, decorate with slices of pineapple and serve.

Cool Cranberries

SOFT FRUITS MAKE WONDERFULLY COLOURFUL AND TASTY DRINKS. THIS IS A GREAT
WAY TO ENCOURAGE YOUR CHILDREN TO EAT MORE FRUIT.

SERVES 4

350 G/12 OZ CRANBERRIES, THAWED
IF FROZEN

425 ML/15 FL OZ CRANBERRY JUICE,
CHILLED

300 ML/10 FL OZ NATURAL YOGURT

2–3 TBSP CLEAR HONEY

Place the berries and juice in the blender and process until smooth. Add th
yogurt and the honey and process again until combined. Taste and add mo
honey if necessary.

Pour into chilled glasses and serve.

Strawberry Colada

STRAWBERRIES ARE A DELICIOUS WAY TO GET YOUR DAILY REQUIREMENT OF IRON, POTASSIUM AND VITAMINS A AND C.

SERVES 2

450 G/1 LB STRAWBERRIES
125 ML/4 FL OZ COCONUT CREAM
600 ML/1 PINT PINEAPPLE JUICE, CHILLED

Reserve 4 strawberries to decorate. Halve the remainder and place in the blender.

Add the coconut cream and pineapple juice and process until smooth, then pour into chilled glasses, decorate with the reserved strawberries and serve.

Watermelon Sunset

THE SEEDS OF A WATERMELON CAN BE ROASTED AND EATEN, AND IN FACT THE RIND CAN

BE USED TO MAKE PICKLES AND RELISHES, MAKING EVERY PART OF THE FRUIT EDIBLE.

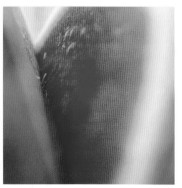 

SERVES 4

1 WATERMELON, HALVED
6 TBSP FRESH RUBY GRAPEFRUIT JUICE
6 TBSP FRESH ORANGE JUICE
DASH OF LIME JUICE

DECORATION
SLICES OF WATERMELON

Deseed the melon if you are unable to find a seedless one. Scoop the flesh into the blender and add the grapefruit juice, orange juice and a dash of li juice.

Process until smooth, pour into chilled glasses, decorate with slices of waterme and serve.

Apple Cooler

THE DISTINCTIVE FLAVOUR OF FRAGRANT, RIPE APPLES COMBINES WITH FRESH STRAWBERRIES AND FRESHLY SQUEEZED ORANGE JUICE TO GIVE YOU A REALLY ZINGY SMOOTHIE.

SERVES 2

2 RIPE APPLES, PEELED
  AND ROUGHLY CHOPPED
55 G/2 OZ STRAWBERRIES, HULLED
JUICE OF 4 ORANGES
SUGAR, TO TASTE

DECORATION
SLICES OF APPLE

Put the apples, strawberries and orange juice into a food processor and process until smooth.

Taste and sweeten with sugar if necessary.

Decorate with slices of apple and serve at once.

Lemon Surprise

ALTHOUGH RICH IN VITAMIN C AND LOW IN CALORIES, LEMON JUICE IS TOO SOUR
TO DRINK ON ITS OWN. HERE IT IS PARTNERED WITH PARSLEY, WHICH ALSO HAS
HEALTH-GIVING PROPERTIES.

SERVES 2

JUICE OF 1 LEMON
1 TBSP CHOPPED FRESH PARSLEY
425 ML/15 FL OZ SPARKLING
  MINERAL WATER
2–3 TSP SUGAR

Put the lemon juice, parsley and mineral water in a blender and process on
low speed until combined.

Switch the blender to high speed, add the sugar through the feeder tube and
process for 30 seconds more.

Pour into chilled glasses, add straws and serve.

Melon & Mint Cooler

THE AROMATIC, SWEET-FLESHED, JUICY CANTALOUPE MELON IS THE PERFECT

CHOICE FOR A REFRESHING AND HEALTHY SUMMER DRINK.

SERVES 2

1 CANTALOUPE MELON
1 TBSP CHOPPED FRESH MINT
1 TBSP CHOPPED STEM GINGER
100–150 ML/3$^{1}/_{2}$–5 FL OZ
  MINERAL WATER

Halve the melon and scoop out and discard the seeds. Scoop out the flesh and chop coarsely.

Put the melon, mint and ginger in a blender and process until smooth and thoroughly combined. With the motor running, add the mineral water, a little at a time, until the mixture reaches the consistency that suits you.

Pour into chilled glasses, add straws and serve.

Maidenly Mimosa

THIS NON-ALCOHOLIC 'COCKTAIL' IS A DELICIOUS ALTERNATIVE FOR NON-DRINKERS
AND DRIVERS AT A BRUNCH OR LUNCH PARTY.

SERVES 2

175 ML/6 FL OZ FRESHLY SQUEEZED
ORANGE JUICE

175 ML/6 FL OZ SPARKLING WHITE
GRAPE JUICE

Divide the orange juice between 2 chilled wine glasses or champagne flute

Top up with the grape juice and serve.

Peach & Redcurrant Sunset

MAKE SURE THE PEACHES YOU USE ARE PROPERLY RIPE SO THEIR FLAVOUR COUNTERACTS THE ACIDITY

OF THE REDCURRANTS. THIS CLASSIC COMBINATION OF FLAVOURS MAKES A VERY PRETTY SMOOTHIE.

 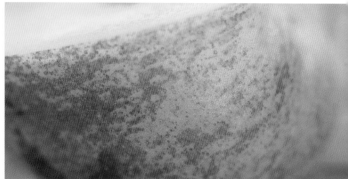

SERVES 2

2 LARGE RIPE PEACHES
100 G/3¹/2 OZ REDCURRANTS
200 ML/7 FL OZ ICE-COLD WATER
1–2 TBSP CLEAR HONEY

Halve the peaches and discard the stones. Roughly chop and put into the food processor.

Keep 2 stems of redcurrants whole for decoration and strip the rest off the stalks into the food processor. Add the water and honey and process until smooth.

Pour into glasses and decorate with the remaining redcurrant sprigs.

Pineapple Crush

THE COMBINATION OF ORANGE JUICE, PINEAPPLE AND MELON MAKES THIS A REALLY
REFRESHING DRINK ON A HOT SUMMER'S DAY.

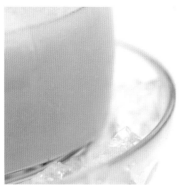 

SERVES 2

100 ML/3½ FL OZ PINEAPPLE JUICE

4 TBSP ORANGE JUICE

125 G/4 OZ GALIA MELON,
    CUT INTO CHUNKS

140 G/5 OZ FROZEN PINEAPPLE CHUNKS

4 ICE CUBES

DECORATION

SLICES OF ORANGE

Pour the pineapple juice and orange juice into a food processor and proces
gently until combined.

Add the melon, pineapple chunks and ice cubes and process until a slushy
consistency has been reached.

Pour the mixture into glasses and decorate with slices of orange. Serve at on

Pomegranate Passion

THIS IS A LOVELY LATE SUMMER DRINK MADE WITH THE NEW SEASON'S POMEGRANATES, WHICH START TO APPEAR IN THE SHOPS IN AUGUST.

SERVES 2

2 RIPE POMEGRANATES
1 PASSION FRUIT
1 TBSP CLEAR HONEY
2 GLASSES FULL OF CRUSHED ICE

Cut the pomegranates in half and extract the juice with an old-fashioned lemon squeezer.

Halve the passion fruit and sieve the pulp into a small bowl. Mix in the pomegranate juice and honey.

Pour over the crushed ice, add a straw and serve.

Raspberry & Apple Quencher

Quick and easy to make, this is a simple and elegant drink to enjoy.

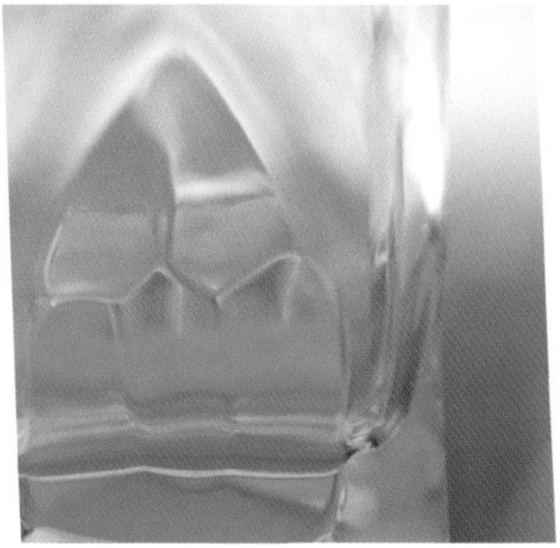

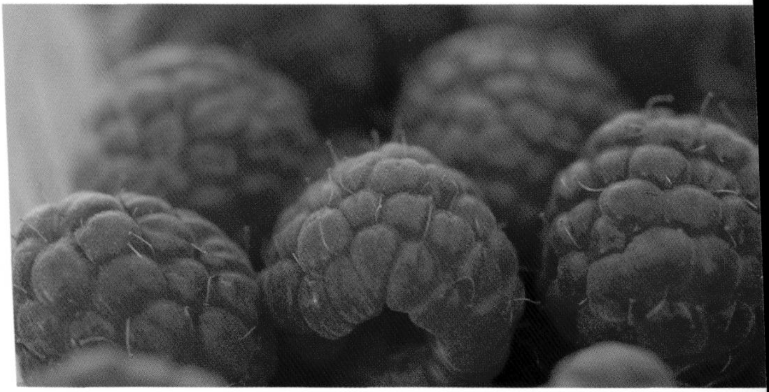

SERVES 2

8 ICE CUBES, CRUSHED
2 TBSP RASPBERRY SYRUP
500 ML/18 FL OZ CHILLED APPLE JUICE

DECORATION
PIECES OF APPLE AND WHOLE RASPBERRIES ON COCKTAIL STICKS

Divide the crushed ice between two glasses and pour over the raspberry syru

Top up each glass with chilled apple juice and stir well.

Decorate with the whole raspberries and pieces of apple on cocktail sticks and serve.

Strawberry Surprise

THIS SUPREMELY THIRST-QUENCHING SMOOTHIE IS IDEAL TO SERVE ON SCORCHING SUMMER

DAYS. THE BALSAMIC VINEGAR BRINGS OUT THE FLAVOUR OF THE STRAWBERRIES BEAUTIFULLY.

SERVES 2

125 G/4^{1}/$_{2}$ OZ FROZEN STRAWBERRIES

200 ML/7 FL OZ ICE-COLD WATER

1 TBSP BALSAMIC VINEGAR

1 TBSP FLOWERY CLEAR HONEY,
    SUCH AS ACACIA

DECORATION

WHOLE STRAWBERRIES

Put the strawberries, water, balsamic vinegar and honey in a food processor and process until smooth.

Pour into glasses, decorate with whole strawberries and serve.

Papaya Sweet & Sour

PAPAYA UNDERGOES AN AMAZING TRANSFORMATION AS IT RIPENS. WITH THE
OUTSIDE SKIN YELLOW, THE SOFT RIPE PAPAYA IS A DEEP SUNSET PINK INSIDE.

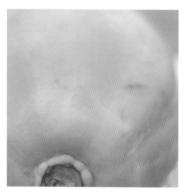 

SERVES 2

250 G/8 OZ RIPE SOFT PAPAYA
200 ML/7 FL OZ ICE-COLD WATER
JUICE OF 1 LIME

DECORATION
SLICES OF GREEN PAPAYA

Peel the ripe papaya, discarding any seeds. Cut into chunks.

Put the papaya chunks into a food processor with the water and lime and
process until smooth.

Pour into glasses and decorate with slices of green papaya.

Black Grape Fizz

USE LARGE DARK GRAPES FOR THIS FOAMY, REFRESHING COOLER.

SERVES 2

125 G/4¹/₂ OZ BLACK GRAPES,
   DESEEDED OR SEEDLESS
200 ML/7 FL OZ SPARKLING
   MINERAL WATER
2 LARGE SCOOPS OF LEMON SORBET

DECORATION
SLICES OF LIME

Put the grapes, mineral water and lemon sorbet in a food processor and process until smooth.

Pour into glasses and decorate with slices of lime. Serve immediately.

Raspberry & Blackcurrant Slush

FRESH, CLEAN AND SIMPLE, THIS IS AN EXCELLENT DRINK TO SERVE ON A REALLY HOT DAY.

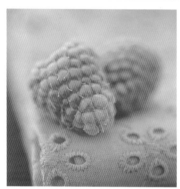

SERVES 2

75 G/2³/4 OZ FROZEN RASPBERRIES

300 ML/10 FL OZ SPARKLING
  MINERAL WATER

2 SCOOPS OF BLACKCURRANT SORBET

Put the raspberries and water into a food processor and process until smooth

Add the sorbet and process briefly until combined with the raspberry mixture

Pour into glasses and drink while still slushy.

Blood Orange Sparkler

Now that blood (ruby) orange juice is available all year round, you can use its fabulous colour and flavour whenever you want.

serves **2**

250 ml/9 fl oz blood (ruby) orange juice

100 g/3¹/₂ oz strawberries

100 g/3¹/₂ oz raspberries

50 ml/2 fl oz sparkling mineral water

Put the blood orange juice, strawberries, raspberries and mineral water into food processor and process until smooth. Sieve the mixture to remove the pips, if preferred.

Pour into glasses, add straws and serve.

Strawberry & Pineapple Refresher

LONG-LIFE PINEAPPLE JUICE AND FROZEN FRUIT ARE USED IN THIS EASY-TO-ASSEMBLE

STORE CUPBOARD SMOOTHIE — THE FLAVOURS ARE NOT COMPROMISED BY YOUR HASTE!

SERVES 2

150 G/5¹/₂ OZ FROZEN STRAWBERRIES
300 ML/10 FL OZ LONG-LIFE
  PINEAPPLE JUICE
1 TBSP CASTER SUGAR

DECORATION
WEDGES OF PINEAPPLE

Put the strawberries, pineapple juice and caster sugar into a food processor and blend until smooth.

Pour into glasses, decorate with wedges of pineapple and serve.

Perfect Pick-Me-Ups

Midsummer Smoothie

SMOOTHIES PROVIDE A QUICK, HEALTHY AND DELICIOUS DRINK THAT'S BOTH
FILLING AND NUTRITIOUS — IDEAL WHEN THERE IS NO TIME TO SIT AND EAT OR AS
A REFRESHING EARLY MORNING STARTER.

SERVES 2

115 G/4 OZ STRAWBERRIES
115 G/4 OZ RASPBERRIES
55 G/2 OZ BLUEBERRIES
1 RIPE PASSION FRUIT
150 ML/5 FL OZ SEMI-SKIMMED MILK

DECORATION
VANILLA AND STRAWBERRY ICE CREAM

Scoop out the passion fruit pulp. Place all the fruits in a juicer or liquidizer
and blend for 1 minute. Add the milk and blend again.

Pour into glasses and serve with a scoop of vanilla and strawberry ice cream
on top of each.

Mango & Orange Smoothie

IF YOU WANT A CREAMY SMOOTHIE, USE VANILLA ICE CREAM INSTEAD OF MANGO
SORBET. THE MANGO MUST BE QUITE RIPE AND FRAGRANT. IT SHOULD BE SOFT
AND YIELD TO GENTLE PRESSURE.

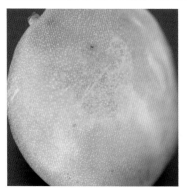 

SERVES 2

1 LARGE RIPE MANGO
JUICE OF 2 MEDIUM ORANGES
3 SCOOPS OF MANGO SORBET

DECORATION
STRIPS OF ORANGE ZEST

Place the mango on a chopping board and cut lengthways through the flesh
as close to the large flat central stone as possible. Turn it over and do the
same thing on the other side of the stone. Remove the peel and roughly chop
the flesh before placing in a processor.

Add the orange juice and sorbet and process until smooth.

Serve at once, decorated with strips of orange zest.

Pear, Orange & Ginger Reviver

PRETTY AND FRAGRANT, WITH THE WARMTH OF GINGER, THIS SMOOTHIE WILL

BRIGHTEN A LESS THAN PERFECT SUMMER'S DAY.

SERVES 2

2 LARGE RIPE WILLIAMS
  OR SIMILAR JUICY PEARS
JUICE OF 4 MEDIUM ORANGES
4 CUBES CRYSTALLIZED GINGER

Peel and quarter the pears, removing the cores. Put into a food processor with the orange juice and the crystallized ginger and process until smooth.

Pour into glasses and serve.

Honeydew

THE NATURAL TEXTURE OF THE HONEYDEW MELON LENDS ITSELF TO THIS
DELICATE SMOOTHIE. FOR BEST RESULTS, MAKE SURE THE MELON IS TRULY RIPE.

SERVES 2

250 G/9 OZ HONEYDEW MELON
300 ML/10 FL OZ SPARKLING
  MINERAL WATER
2 TBSP CLEAR HONEY

DECORATION
REDCURRANT CLUSTERS

Cut the rind off the melon. Chop the melon into chunks, discarding any seeds

Put into a food processor with the water and honey and process until smooth

Pour into glasses and decorate with clusters of redcurrants.

Summer Fruit Slush

THIS MEDLEY OF SUMMER BERRIES MAKES AN INSPIRED DRINK.

SERVES 2

4 TBSP ORANGE JUICE

1 TBSP LIME JUICE

100 ML/3 ¹/2 FL OZ SPARKLING WATER

350 G/12 OZ FROZEN SUMMER
FRUITS (SUCH AS BLUEBERRIES,
RASPBERRIES, BLACKBERRIES AND
STRAWBERRIES)

4 ICE CUBES

Pour the orange juice, lime juice and sparkling water into a food processor and process gently until combined.

Add the summer fruits and ice cubes and process until a slushy consistency has been reached.

Pour the mixture into glasses and serve.

Forest Fruit Smoothie

THIS DRINK COMBINES THE RICH FLAVOURS AND COLOURS OF FOREST FRUITS IN

ONE SUPERB SMOOTHIE.

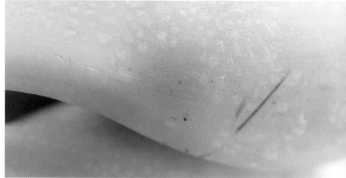

SERVES 2

350 ML/12 FL OZ ORANGE JUICE

1 BANANA, SLICED AND FROZEN

450 G/1 LB FROZEN FOREST FRUITS

  (SUCH AS BLUEBERRIES, RASPBERRIES

  AND BLACKBERRIES)

DECORATION

SLICES OF ORANGE

Pour the orange juice into a food processor. Add the banana and half of the forest fruits and process until smooth.

Add the remaining forest fruits and process until smooth. Pour the mixture into tall glasses and decorate the rims with slices of orange.

Add straws and serve.

Melon Refresher

INCORPORATING THREE DIFFERENT TYPES OF MELONS, THE FLAVOUR OF THIS
SMOOTHIE IS BOTH DELICATE AND REFRESHING ON A HOT DAY.

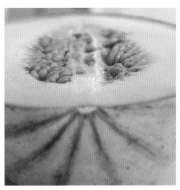

SERVES 2

250 ML/9 FL OZ NATURAL YOGURT

100 G/3¹/2 OZ GALIA MELON,
  CUT INTO CHUNKS

100 G/3¹/2 OZ CANTALOUPE MELON,
  CUT INTO CHUNKS

100 G/3¹/2 OZ WATERMELON,
  CUT INTO CHUNKS

6 ICE CUBES

DECORATION
WEDGES OF MELON

Pour the yogurt into a food processor. Add the galia melon chunks and
process until smooth.

Add the cantaloupe and watermelon chunks along with the ice cubes and
process until smooth.

Pour the mixture into glasses and decorate with wedges of melon.

Serve at once.

Homemade Lemonade

THIS CLASSIC COOLER IS A WELL-LOVED, TRADITIONAL FAVOURITE.

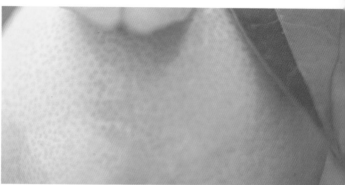

SERVES 2

150 ML/5 FL OZ WATER
6 TBSP SUGAR
1 TSP GRATED LEMON RIND
125 ML/4 FL OZ LEMON JUICE
6 ICE CUBES

TO SERVE
SPARKLING WATER

DECORATION
GRANULATED SUGAR
SLICES OF LEMON

Put the water, sugar and grated lemon rind into a small saucepan and bring to the boil, stirring constantly. Continue to boil, stirring, for 5 minutes.

Remove from the heat and leave to cool to room temperature. Stir in the lemon juice, then transfer to a jug, cover with clingfilm and chill in the refrigerator for at least 2 hours.

When the lemonade has almost finished chilling, take two glasses and rub the rims with a wedge of lemon, then dip them in granulated sugar to frost Put the ice cubes into the glasses.

Remove the lemon syrup from the refrigerator, pour it over the ice and top up with sparkling water. The ratio should be one part lemon syrup to three parts sparkling water. Stir well to mix, decorate with sugar and slices of fre lemon and serve.

Cranberry Energizer

SWEET AND SOUR COMBINE TO MAKE A DELICIOUSLY ENERGIZING JUICE PACKED
FULL OF GOODNESS.

SERVES 2

300 ML/10 FL OZ CRANBERRY JUICE
100 ML/3¹/₂ FL OZ ORANGE JUICE
150 G/5¹/₂ OZ FRESH RASPBERRIES
1 TBSP LEMON JUICE

DECORATION
SLICES AND SPIRALS OF FRESH
  LEMON OR ORANGE

Pour the cranberry juice and orange juice into a food processor and process gen
until combined. Add the raspberries and lemon juice and process until smoo

Pour the mixture into glasses and decorate with slices and spirals of fresh
lemon or orange. Serve at once.

Cherry Sour

USE THE BOTTLING LIQUID AS WELL AS THE FRUIT FOR THIS SHARP,

THIRST-QUENCHING SMOOTHIE.

SERVES 2

250 G/9 OZ BOTTLED MORELLO
   CHERRIES

150 ML/5 FL OZ GREEK YOGURT

SUGAR, TO TASTE

DECORATION

CHERRIES ON COCKTAIL STICKS

Put the cherries with their bottling liquid into a food processor with the yogurt and process until smooth.

Taste and sweeten with sugar if necessary.

Pour into glasses and serve. Decorate with cherries on a cocktail stick.

Banana & Apple Booster

GINGER AND CINNAMON SPICE UP THESE EVERYDAY FRUITS TO MAKE A GREAT ENERGIZER FOR A COLD WINTER'S MORNING.

 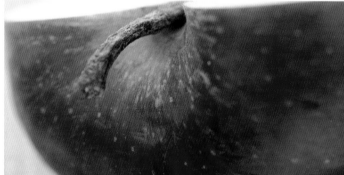

SERVES 2

250 ML/9 FL OZ APPLE JUICE
1/2 TSP POWDERED CINNAMON
2 TSP GRATED FRESH ROOT GINGER
2 BANANAS, SLICED AND FROZEN

DECORATION
CHUNKS OF FRESH APPLE ON
   COCKTAIL STICKS

Pour the apple juice into a food processor. Add the cinnamon and ginger a process gently until combined.

Add the bananas and process until smooth. Pour the mixture into glasses a decorate with chunks of fresh apple on cocktail sticks. Serve at once.

Blackcurrant Bracer

PURPLE PASSION! FOR A STRICTLY GROWN-UP VERSION, USE CRÈME DE CASSIS INSTEAD OF THE CORDIAL.

SERVES 2

100 G/3¹/₂ OZ FROZEN BLACKCURRANTS

4 SCOOPS OF BLACKCURRANT SORBET

100 ML/3¹/₂ FL OZ CRÈME FRAÎCHE

2 TBSP BLACKCURRANT CORDIAL,
PLUS EXTRA FOR DRIZZLING

1 TBSP WATER

SUGAR, TO TASTE

DECORATION

A FEW MINT LEAVES

WHOLE BLACKBERRIES

Put the blackcurrants, sorbet, crème fraîche, cordial and water into a food processor and process until smooth. Taste and sweeten with a little sugar if necessary.

Pour into glasses. Drizzle over some cordial, decorate with the mint leaves and blackberries and serve.

Kiwi Cooler

USE A STRAWBERRY ICE CREAM TO CONTRAST WITH THE GLORIOUS GREEN COLOUR OF THIS SMOOTHIE, OR A LIME SORBET TO TONE IN WITH IT. WHICHEVER YOU CHOOSE, THE COMBINATION WILL BE DELIGHTFUL.

SERVES 2

4 RIPE KIWI FRUIT,
  PEELED AND QUARTERED
200 ML/7 FL OZ TRADITIONAL
  SPARKLING LEMONADE

DECORATION
2 LARGE SCOOPS OF ICE CREAM
  OR SORBET

Put the kiwi fruit and lemonade into a food processor and process until smooth

Pour into glasses and top with a scoop of ice cream or sorbet.

Serve at once.

Pineapple Tango

THIS LONG, COOL, THIRST-QUENCHER WILL REVITALIZE YOU WHEN YOU ARE

FEELING TIRED OR STRESSED.

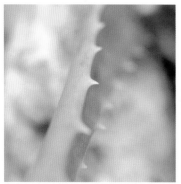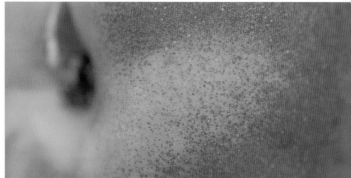

SERVES 2

125 ML/4 FL OZ PINEAPPLE JUICE
JUICE OF 1 LEMON
100 ML/3¹/2 FL OZ WATER
3 TBSP BROWN SUGAR
175 ML/6 FL OZ NATURAL YOGURT
1 PEACH, CUT INTO CHUNKS AND FROZEN
100 G/3¹/2 OZ FROZEN
   PINEAPPLE CHUNKS

Pour the pineapple juice, lemon juice and water into a food processor. Add the sugar and yogurt and process until blended.

Add the peach and pineapple chunks and process until smooth.

Pour the mixture into glasses and decorate the rims with wedges of fresh pineapp.

Serve at once.

DECORATION
WEDGES OF FRESH PINEAPPLE

Cherry Kiss

A GREAT PARTY DRINK FOR THOSE AVOIDING ALCOHOL, THIS CHERRY DRINK
TASTES AS GOOD AS IT LOOKS.

 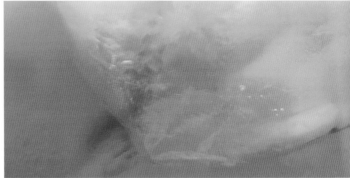

SERVES 2

8 ICE CUBES, CRUSHED

2 TBSP CHERRY SYRUP

500 ML/18 FL OZ SPARKLING WATER

DECORATION

MARASCHINO CHERRIES ON LONG
  SWIZZLE STICKS

Divide the crushed ice between two glasses and pour over the cherry syrup.

Top up each glass with sparkling water. Decorate with the maraschino
cherries on long swizzle sticks and serve.

White Grape Elderflower Foam

USE CHAMPAGNE OR MUSCAT GRAPES TO ADD TO THE DELICATE FLOWERINESS OF

THIS LIGHT SMOOTHIE.

 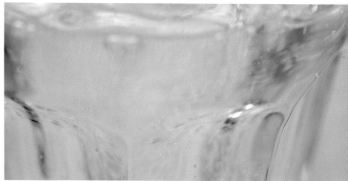

SERVES 2

125 G/4¹/2 OZ WHITE GRAPES,
   DESEEDED OR SEEDLESS
200 ML/7 FL OZ SPARKLING
   MINERAL WATER
2 LARGE SCOOPS OF
   FROZEN YOGURT (PLAIN)
1¹/2 TBSP ELDERFLOWER CORDIAL

DECORATION
WHITE GRAPES

Put the grapes, mineral water, frozen yogurt and elderflower cordial in a fo
processor and process until smooth.

Pour into glasses, add a few grapes and serve immediately.

Elderflower & Pear Smoothie

MAKE THIS SMOOTHIE IN LATE SPRING OR EARLY SUMMER WHEN THE ELDER BUSHES
ARE IN FULL BLOOM.

SERVES 2

4 SMALL FIRM PEARS

2 HEADS OF ELDER FLOWERS,
FRESHLY PICKED (OR A DASH
OF CORDIAL)

1 STRIP OF LEMON ZEST

1 TBSP SOFT BROWN SUGAR

4 TBSP WATER

200 ML/7 FL OZ SEMI-SKIMMED MILK

TO SERVE
LANGUES DE CHAT BISCUITS

Peel and quarter the pears, discarding the cores. Place in a saucepan with t
elder flowers, a strip of lemon zest, the sugar and water. Cover tightly and
simmer until the pears are very soft. Allow to cool.

Discard the elder flowers and lemon zest. Put the pears, cooking liquid and
milk into a food processor and process until smooth.

Serve immediately with langues de chat biscuits.

Fig & Maple Melter

GO ON, INDULGE YOURSELF IN THIS RICH, DELICIOUS AND SOPHISTICATED SMOOTHIE.

SERVES 2

350 ML/12 FL OZ HAZELNUT
  YOGURT
2 TBSP FRESHLY SQUEEZED
  ORANGE JUICE
4 TBSP MAPLE SYRUP
8 LARGE FRESH FIGS, CHOPPED
6 ICE CUBES

DECORATION
TOASTED CHOPPED HAZELNUTS

Pour the yogurt, orange juice and maple syrup into a food processor and process gently until combined.

Add the figs and ice cubes and process until smooth.

Pour the mixture into glasses and scatter over some toasted chopped hazelnu

Serve at once.

Green Tea & Yellow Plum Smoothie

THE HAUNTING FLAVOUR OF GREEN TEA COMBINES BRILLIANTLY WITH GOLDEN-YELLOW PLUMS. IF THE WEATHER ISN'T WONDERFUL, THIS SMOOTHIE IS JUST AS DELICIOUS SERVED WARM.

SERVES 2

1 GREEN TEA WITH ORIENTAL
   SPICE TEA BAG
300 ML/10 FL OZ BOILING WATER
1 TBSP SUGAR
125 G/4¹/2 OZ RIPE YELLOW PLUMS,
   HALVED AND STONED

Put the tea bag in a teapot or jug and pour over the boiling water. Leave to infuse for 7 minutes. Remove and discard the tea bag. Allow to cool, then chill.

Pour the chilled tea into a food processor. Add the sugar and plums and process until smooth.

Serve at once.

Super Shakes

Chocolate Milkshake

THE ULTIMATE MILKSHAKE FOR CHILDREN AND CHOCOHOLICS ALIKE, THIS DRINK IS
SUPREMELY SATISFYING.

 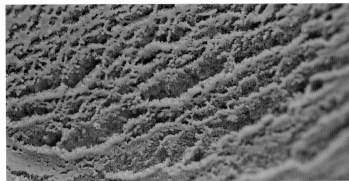

SERVES 2

150 ML/5 FL OZ MILK

2 TBSP CHOCOLATE SYRUP

400 G/14 OZ CHOCOLATE ICE CREAM

DECORATION

GRATED CHOCOLATE

Pour the milk and chocolate syrup into a food processor and process gently until combined.

Add the chocolate ice cream and process until smooth. Pour the mixture int tall glasses and scatter the grated chocolate over the shakes.

Serve at once.

Spiced Banana Milkshake

THIS IS A CARIBBEAN COMBINATION OF FRUIT AND SPICES THAT WILL TANTALIZE
THE TASTEBUDS.

SERVES 2

300 ML/10 FL OZ MILK
1/2 TSP MIXED SPICE
150 G/5 1/2 OZ BANANA ICE CREAM
2 BANANAS, SLICED AND FROZEN

DECORATION
PINCH OF MIXED SPICE

Pour the milk into a food processor and add the mixed spice. Add half of the banana ice cream and process gently until combined, then add the remaining ice cream and process until well blended.

When the mixture is well combined, add the bananas and process until smooth.

Pour the mixture into glasses, add a pinch of mixed spice to decorate and serve.

Strawberries & Cream Milkshake

THE ULTIMATE STRAWBERRY MILKSHAKE! FORGET ABOUT SYNTHETIC STRAWBERRY-FLAVOURED SYRUPS — THIS IS THE REAL THING: A GORGEOUS FLAVOUR AND FANTASTICALLY FRUITY. SET OFF THE PALE COLOURING WITH SOME PRETTY GREEN MINT LEAVES.

SERVES 2

150 G/5$^1/_2$ OZ FROZEN
  STRAWBERRIES
100 ML/3$^1/_2$ FL OZ SINGLE CREAM
200 ML/7 FL OZ COLD
  FULL-CREAM MILK
1 TBSP CASTER SUGAR

DECORATION
MINT LEAVES

Put the strawberries, cream, milk and caster sugar into a food processor and process until smooth.

Pour into glasses and serve decorated with mint leaves.

Smooth Nectarine Shake

Mango and nectarine is an inspired combination of fruits, made all the more special with the clever addition of lemon sorbet.

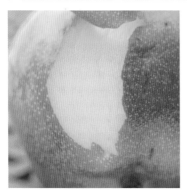

SERVES 2

250 ML/9 FL OZ MILK
350 G/12 OZ LEMON SORBET
1 RIPE MANGO, STONED AND DICED
2 RIPE NECTARINES, STONED
   AND DICED

DECORATION
THIN WEDGES OF NECTARINE

Pour the milk into a food processor, add half of the lemon sorbet and proce
gently until combined. Add the remaining sorbet and process until smooth.

When the mixture is thoroughly blended, gradually add the mango and
nectarines and process until smooth.

Pour the mixture into glasses, decorate with thin wedges of nectarine and serv

Tropical Storm

REVIVE YOURSELF WITH THIS INVIGORATING AND EXUBERANT TROPICAL SHAKE.

SERVES 2

250 ML/9 FL OZ MILK

50 ML/2 FL OZ COCONUT MILK

150 G/5¹/2 OZ VANILLA ICE CREAM

2 BANANAS, SLICED AND FROZEN

200 G/7 OZ CANNED PINEAPPLE
 CHUNKS, DRAINED

1 PAPAYA, DESEEDED AND DICED

DECORATION

GRATED COCONUT

Pour the milk and coconut milk into a food processor and process gently until combined. Add half of the ice cream and process gently, then add the remaining ice cream and process until smooth.

Add the bananas and process well, then add the pineapple chunks and papaya and process until smooth.

Pour the mixture into tall glasses and scatter the grated coconut over the top and serve.

Peach Bliss

DIFFERENT FRUITS COMBINE WITH PEACHES TO MAKE ONE MARVELLOUSLY

FRUITY DRINK.

SERVES 2

175 ML/6 FL OZ MILK

225 G/8 OZ CANNED
    PEACH SLICES, DRAINED

2 FRESH APRICOTS, CHOPPED

400 G/14 OZ FRESH STRAWBERRIES,
    HULLED AND SLICED

2 BANANAS, SLICED AND FROZEN

DECORATION

SLICES OF NECTARINE, STRAWBERRIES
AND BANANA ON COCKTAIL STICKS

Pour the milk into a food processor. Add the peach slices and process gently until combined. Add the apricots and process gently until combined.

Add the strawberries and banana slices and process until smooth.

Pour the mixture into glasses and decorate with the fruit speared on a cocktail stick.

Serve at once.

Perfect Plum Shake

A DEEP, RICH AND FRUITY SHAKE FOR THE END OF THE SUMMER.

SERVES 2

250 G/9 OZ RIPE DAMSONS
200 ML/7 FL OZ WATER
1 TBSP GOLDEN GRANULATED SUGAR
4 SCOOPS OF FROZEN YOGURT
  (PLAIN) OR ICE CREAM

DECORATION
2 ITALIAN ALMOND OR PISTACHIO
  BISCOTTI, CRUMBLED
PLUMS, WHOLE OR CUT IN HALF

Put the damsons, water and sugar into a small saucepan. Cover tightly and simmer for about 15 minutes, until the damsons have split and are very soft. Allow to cool.

Strain off the liquid into a food processor and add the frozen yogurt or ice cream. Process until smooth and frothy.

Pour into glasses and decorate the rims with whole or halved plums. Sprinkle with the crumbled biscotti and serve.

Raspberry Ripple Rice Cream

A FRESH-TASTING, NON-DAIRY SHAKE WITH NO ANIMAL PRODUCTS, NO CHOLESTEROL, NO
LACTOSE AND NO PROBLEM! RICE 'MILK' SHOULD BE KEPT COLD IN THE FRIDGE FOR THE BEST-
TASTING RESULTS. SOYA MILK CAN BE USED INSTEAD, BUT THE RICE 'MILK' TASTES MUCH NICER.

SERVES 2

125 G/4¹/₂ OZ FROZEN RASPBERRIES
300 ML/10 FL OZ RICE 'MILK'
OR SOYA MILK

Put the raspberries and half the rice 'milk' into a food processor and process
until smooth.

Strain into a jug and carefully stir through the remaining rice 'milk' to give a
marbled effect.

Pour into glasses and serve.

Coffee Banana Cooler

A POWERHOUSE FOR THOSE WHO LEAD AN ACTIVE LIFE — THIS MILKSHAKE TASTES

FABULOUS, TOO.

SERVES 2

300 ML/10 FL OZ MILK
4 TBSP INSTANT COFFEE POWDER
150 G/5^1/$_2$ OZ VANILLA ICE CREAM
2 BANANAS, SLICED AND FROZEN

Pour the milk into a food processor, add the coffee powder and process gently until combined. Add half of the vanilla ice cream and process gently, then add the remaining ice cream and process until well combined.

When the mixture is thoroughly blended, add the bananas and process until smooth.

Pour the mixture into glasses and serve.

Plum Fluff

You will need perfectly ripe plums for this fabulously frothy, fruity recipe. Dark ones – such as Marjorie's Seedling – give a better colour.

SERVES 2

4 MEDIUM RIPE PLUMS, STONED
200 ML/7 FL OZ ICE-COLD MILK
2 SCOOPS OF LUXURY VANILLA
  ICE CREAM

TO SERVE
CRUMBLY OAT BISCUITS

Put the plums, milk and ice cream into a food processor and process until smooth and frothy.

Pour into glasses and serve at once with crumbly oat biscuits.

Peach & Orange Milkshake

A LUSCIOUS COMBINATION OF FRUITS TO LEAVE YOU RESTORED, REVIVED AND REFRESHED.

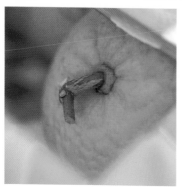 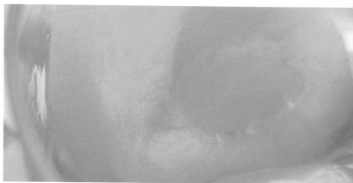

SERVES 2

100 ML/3¹/₂ FL OZ MILK
125 ML/4 FL OZ PEACH YOGURT
100 ML/3¹/₂ FL OZ ORANGE JUICE
225 G/8 OZ CANNED PEACH SLICES,
   DRAINED
6 ICE CUBES

DECORATION
STRIPS OF ORANGE PEEL

Pour the milk, yogurt and orange juice into a food processor and process gently until combined.

Add the peach slices and ice cubes and process until smooth. Pour the mixture into glasses and decorate with strips of orange peel.

Black & White Smoothie

CHOCOLATE AND CHERRIES ARE A CLASSIC COMBINATION. YOU CAN ALSO SERVE
THIS WHITE CHOCOLATE AND BLACK CHERRY SMOOTHIE AS A DESSERT, WITH A
COUPLE OF DARK CHOCOLATE THINS.

SERVES 2

150 G/5^{1}/$_{2}$ OZ BLACK CHERRIES
3 LARGE SCOOPS OF LUXURY
  WHITE CHOCOLATE ICE CREAM
150 ML/5 FL OZ MILK

Halve and stone the black cherries. Put these into a food processor and
process until puréed.

Add the ice cream and milk and process briefly to mix well.

Pour into glasses and serve.

Creamy Maple Shake

MAPLE, VANILLA AND ALMOND ARE DELICATE FLAVOURS THAT COMPLEMENT EACH

OTHER PERFECTLY.

SERVES 2

150 ML/5 FL OZ MILK
2 TBSP MAPLE SYRUP
400 G/14 OZ VANILLA ICE CREAM
1 TBSP ALMOND ESSENCE

DECORATION
CHOPPED ALMONDS

Pour the milk and maple syrup into a food processor and process gently until combined.

Add the ice cream and almond essence and process until smooth.

Pour the mixture into glasses, scatter the chopped nuts over the shakes and serve.

Kiwi & Lime Shake

THIS DRINK PROVIDES A GOOD SOURCE OF VITAMIN C, AS WELL AS A WONDERFULLY
REFRESHING SWEET AND SHARP FLAVOUR.

SERVES 2

150 ML/5 FL OZ MILK
JUICE OF 2 LIMES
2 KIWI FRUIT, CHOPPED
1 TBSP SUGAR
400 G/14 OZ VANILLA ICE CREAM

DECORATION
SLICES OF KIWI FRUIT
STRIPS OF LIME PEEL

Pour the milk and lime juice into a food processor and process gently until combined

Add the kiwi fruit and sugar and process gently, then add the ice cream and
process until smooth.

Pour the mixture into glasses and decorate with slices of kiwi fruit and strip
of lime peel.

Serve at once.

Peppermint Refresher

SURPRISINGLY BOTH HOT AND COLD ON THE TONGUE, THIS MINTY COOLER WILL
RESTORE VITALITY AND VIGOUR.

SERVES 2

150 ML/5 FL OZ MILK
2 TBSP PEPPERMINT SYRUP
400 G/14 OZ PEPPERMINT ICE CREAM

DECORATION
SPRIGS OF FRESH MINT

Pour the milk and peppermint syrup into a food processor and process gently
until combined.

Add the peppermint ice cream and process until smooth.

Pour the mixture into tall glasses and decorate with sprigs of fresh mint.

Coconut Cream

AN INVIGORATING AND CREAMY SMOOTHIE TO LIFT YOUR MOOD AND REMIND
YOU OF TROPICAL BEACHES.

SERVES 2

350 ML/12 FL OZ PINEAPPLE JUICE
90 ML/3¹/₄ FL OZ COCONUT MILK
150 G/5¹/₂ OZ VANILLA ICE CREAM
140 G/5 OZ FROZEN PINEAPPLE CHUNKS

DECORATION
2 TBSP GRATED FRESH COCONUT

TO SERVE
2 SCOOPED-OUT COCONUT SHELLS,
  OPTIONAL

Pour the pineapple juice and coconut milk into a food processor. Add the ice cream and process until smooth.

Add the pineapple chunks and process until smooth.

Pour the mixture into scooped-out coconut shells, or tall glasses, and decorate with grated fresh coconut.

Add straws and serve.

Fuzzy Peg

A CHILD'S DELIGHT BOTH IN TASTE AND ITS INCREDIBLY STRANGE APPEARANCE! IT
COULD BE MADE WITH OTHER DRINKS TOO.

 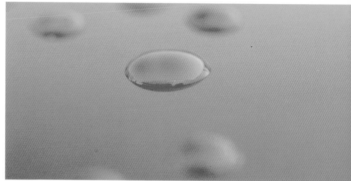

SERVES 1

2 SCOOPS VANILLA ICE CREAM
1 MEASURE LIME OR LEMON JUICE
  CORDIAL
COLA
ICE

Blend the ice cream and lime or lemon cordial together for 5–10 seconds with a
little cola.

Pour into a tall glass filled with ice and top up with cola.

Drink through straws.

Mocha Cream

THE HEAVENLY PAIRING OF COFFEE AND CHOCOLATE CAN BE IMPROVED ONLY BY
THE ADDITION OF WHIPPED CREAM.

SERVES 2

200 ML/7 FL OZ MILK

50 ML/2 FL OZ SINGLE CREAM

1 TBSP BROWN SUGAR

2 TBSP COCOA POWDER

1 TBSP COFFEE SYRUP OR INSTANT
  COFFEE POWDER

6 ICE CUBES

DECORATION

WHIPPED CREAM

GRATED CHOCOLATE

Put the milk, cream and sugar into a food processor and process gently
until combined.

Add the cocoa powder and coffee syrup or powder and process well, then add
the ice cubes and process until smooth.

Pour the mixture into glasses. Top with whipped cream, scatter the grated
chocolate over the drinks and serve.

Iced Coffee & Chocolate Crush

COFFEE AND A HINT OF PEPPERMINT COMBINE IN THIS DELICIOUS CRUSH, WHICH IS
TOPPED WITH CHOCOLATE.

SERVES 2

400 ML/14 FL OZ MILK
200 ML/7 FL OZ COFFEE SYRUP
100 ML/3¹/2 FL OZ PEPPERMINT SYRUP
1 TBSP CHOPPED FRESH MINT LEAVES
4 ICE CUBES

DECORATION
GRATED CHOCOLATE
SPRIGS OF FRESH MINT

Pour the milk, coffee syrup and peppermint syrup into a food processor and process gently until combined.

Add the mint and ice cubes and process until a slushy consistency has been reached.

Pour the mixture into glasses. Scatter over the grated chocolate, decorate with sprigs of fresh mint and serve.

index